Animals I Will Find at the Zoo

ORANGUTAN

Shannon Anderson

Table of Contents

A Starfish Book

SEAHORSE PUBLISHING

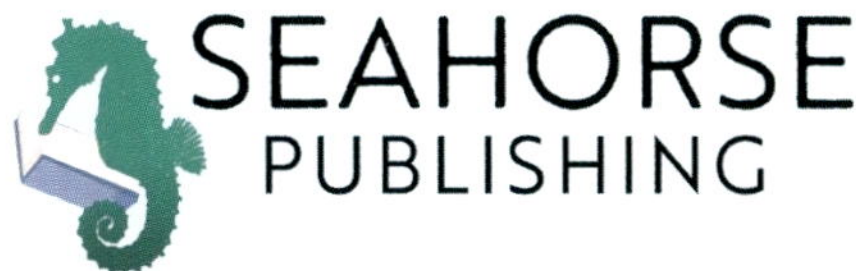

Teaching Tips for Caregivers:

As a caregiver, you can help your child succeed in school by giving them a strong foundation in language and literacy skills and a desire to learn to read.

This book helps children grow by letting them practice reading skills.

Reading for pleasure and interest will help your child to develop reading skills and will give your child the opportunity to practice these skills in meaningful ways.

- Encourage your child to read on her own at home
- Encourage your child to practice reading aloud
- Encourage activities that require reading
- Establish a reading time
- Talk with your child
- Give your child writing materials

Teaching Tips for Teachers:

Research shows that one of the best ways for students to learn a new topic is to read about it.

Before Reading

- Read the "Words to Know" and discuss the meaning of each word.
- Read the back cover to see what the book is about.

During Reading

- When a student gets to a word that is unknown, ask them to look at the rest of the sentence to find clues to help with the meaning of the unknown word.
- Ask the student to write down any pages of the book that were confusing to them.

After Reading

- Discuss the main idea of the book.
- Ask students to give one detail that they learned in the book by showing a text dependent answer from the book.

ORANGUTAN

A zoo is a fun place to see animals and learn about them.

One animal you may find in a zoo is an orangutan.

Orangutans are the largest animals that live in trees.

They are **primates**.

They belong to the ape family.

Humans are primates, too. That means we are related to orangutans!

Orangutans have red hair.

Their arms are longer than their legs.

They are very good at climbing and moving around in trees.

An orangutan’s favorite food is fruit.

Orangutans also eat seeds, bark, and sometimes insects.

Orangutans mostly like to live alone.

But orangutan moms stay with their babies and care for them for many years.

An orangutan baby is called a "baby," just like humans.

Orangutans are **mammals**, so babies drink their mom's milk.

The mom carries her baby around with her.

She teaches her baby how to find food and build a nest for sleeping.

Orangutans are smart.

They use sticks as tools to help them get and eat food.

Orangutans teach each other to use tools.

Orangutans make noises and move their bodies to **communicate**.

Some of their sounds are barks, squeaks, and screams.

Some orangutans have learned sign language from humans.

NORTH AMERICA

EUROPE

ASIA

AFRICA

SOUTH AMERICA

AUSTRALIA

Orangutans live in **rainforests** on two islands in **Asia**.

If you cannot go to Asia to see orangutans, you can find them at the zoo!

Words to Know

Asia (AY-zhuh): one of Earth's continents; a very large landmass in Earth's eastern hemisphere north of the equator

communicate (kuh-MYOO-ni-kate): to share information, feelings, or ideas with others

mammals (MAM-uhlz): animals that have hair or fur, that give birth to live babies, and that make milk to feed their babies

primates (PRYE-mates): members of the group of mammals that includes monkeys, apes, and people

rainforests (RAYN-for-ists): forests in tropical regions of the world where it rains a lot

Index

Comprehension Questions

1. What kind of mammal is an orangutan?
   a. a marsupial b. a rodent c. a primate

2. What do orangutans like to eat the most?
   a. fruit b. frogs c. snakes

3. Baby orangutans are called ____.
   a. babies b. cubs c. monkeys

4. True or False: Orangutans like to live in big groups.

5. True or False: Orangutans are good at moving around in caves.

Answers
1. c 2. a 3. a 4. False 5. False

About the Author

Shannon Anderson is an award-winning children's book author and former elementary school teacher. She loves animals and has eight pets of her own. You can learn more about her or invite her to your school at www.shannonisteaching.com.

Written by: Shannon Anderson
Design by: Under the Oaks Media
Editor: Kim Thompson

Photographs/Shutterstock: Gudkov Andrey: cover; Don Mammoser: p. 3; Asia Travel: p. 5; Stephen Lavery: p. 6; Kylie Nicholson: p. 9; Katesalin Pagkaihang: p. 10; Capatin Al: p. 12; Sergio Bertino: p. 13; lukaZemanphoto: p. 14; Ricky Santana: p. 15

Library of Congress PCN Data
Orangutan / Shannon Anderson
Animals I Will Find at the Zoo
ISBN 979-8-8873-5351-7 (hard cover)
ISBN 979-8-8873-5436-1 (paperback)
ISBN 979-8-8873-5521-4 (EPUB)
ISBN 979-8-8873-5606-8 (eBook)
Library of Congress Control Number: 2022949028

Printed in the United States of America.

Seahorse Publishing Company
www.seahorsepub.com

Published in the United States
Seahorse Publishing
PO Box 771325
Coral Springs, FL 33077